BABY ANIMALS
OF THE FROZEN TUNDRA

Carmen Bredeson

Dennis L. Claussen, Ph.D., *Series Science Consultant* Professor of Zoology, Miami University, Oxford, Ohio

Allan A. De Fina, Ph.D., *Series Literacy Consultant* Past President of the New Jersey Reading Association, Chairperson, Department of Literacy Education, New Jersey City University, Jersey City, New Jersey

CONTENTS

WORDS TO KNOW

arctic (ARK tihk)—From the area around the North Pole.

endangered [en DAYN jurd] **animal**—A type of animal that may disappear from Earth.

herds [hurdz]—Groups of plant-eating animals that live together.

pack [pak]—A group of meat-eating animals that live together.

WHERE IS THE TUNDRA?

3　☐ = TUNDRA

TUNDRA

The tundra is very cold. Grasses and small plants grow, but there are no trees. The ground is frozen most of the year. The tundra is home to many animals. Baby animals have special ways to stay safe and live in the tundra.

BABY
ARCTIC FOX

Arctic fox pups are born in the spring. Their fur is brown like the grass. During the winter, the thick fur turns white. It helps them match the snow to stay safe from enemies. The foxes curl up in their bushy tails to stay warm.

A baby musk ox is called a calf. It crawls under its mother's long fur to keep warm. When danger is near, the adults make a circle around the calf. They point their sharp horns out to scare animals away.

BABY **MUSK OX**

BABY SNOWY OWL

Baby snowy owls hatch from eggs. Their parents bring food to the hungry chicks.

While the parents are away, the chicks stay VERY, VERY quiet. That is so wolves and foxes cannot find the chicks.

Wolves live in groups called **packs**. When cubs are born, the whole pack helps care for them. Wolves howl to each other. Sometimes the howl means danger is near.

Baby arctic wolves
are called cubs.

BABY
ARCTIC WOLF

BABY
DALL SHEEP

Dall lambs are born high up on a cliff. They stay safe from wolves and bears up there. As the lambs get bigger, their horns grow. The horns are made of the same thing as your fingernails.

Arctic tern chicks are very hungry. Their parents bring fish and insects for the chicks to eat. Arctic terns spend much of their time in the air. They fly from the North Pole to the South Pole and back EVERY year.

BABY **ARCTIC TERN**

A baby caribou is called a calf.

BABY CARIBOU

A caribou (KA rih boo) calf stands up just after it is born. Very soon the calf can walk. Caribou live in huge **herds**. They move from place to place eating grass. Calves must be able to move with the herd.

Tiny polar bear cubs tumble and play in the snow. Their fur is the same color as the snow. Today, the ice where the polar bears hunt is melting. It is getting harder and harder for the bears to find food.

ENDANGERED ANIMAL OF THE TUNDRA

BABY POLAR BEAR

Learn More

Books

Glassman, Jackie. *Amazing Arctic Animals*.
  New York: Grosset & Dunlap, 2002.

Loughran, Donna. *Living in the Tundra*. New York:
  Children's Press, 2004.

Townsend, Emily Rose. *Arctic Foxes*. Mankato,
  Minn.: Capstone Press, 2006.

Enchanted Learning
http://www.enchantedlearning.com/
  Click on "Biomes." Then click on "Tundra."

National Geographic for Kids
http://kids.nationalgeographic.com/
  Click on "Animals." Then click on "Creature
  Feature." Then click on "Polar Bears"
  or "Snowy Owl."

INDEX

~To our little Texans~Andrew, Charlie, and Kate~

Enslow Elementary, an imprint of Enslow Publishers, Inc.
Enslow Elementary® is a registered trademark of Enslow Publishers, Inc.

Copyright © 2009 by Carmen Bredeson

Library of Congress Cataloging-in-Publication Data

Bredeson, Carmen.
Baby animals of the frozen tundra / Carmen Bredeson.
    p. cm. — (Nature's baby animals)
    Summary: "Up-close photos and information about baby animals of the tundra biome"—Provided by publisher.
    Includes bibliographical references and index.
    ISBN-13: 978-0-7660-3002-2
    ISBN-10: 0-7660-3002-4
    1. Tundra animals—Infancy—Arctic regions—Juvenile literature. I. Title.
    QL105.B74 2009
    591.75'86—dc22

                                                    2007039472

Printed in the United States of America

10 9 8 7 6 5 4 3 2 1

Note to Parents and Teachers: The *Nature's Baby Animals* series supports the National Science Education Standards for K–4 science. The Words to Know section introduces subject-specific vocabulary words, including pronunciation and definitions. Early readers may need help with these new words.

To Our Readers: We have done our best to make sure all Internet addresses in this book were active and appropriate when we went to press. However, the author and the publisher have no control over and assume no liability for the material available on those Internet sites or on other Web sites they may link to. Any comments or suggestions can be sent by e-mail to comments@enslow.com or to the address on the back cover.

Every effort has been made to locate all copyright holders of material used in this book. If any errors or omissions have occurred, corrections will be made in future editions of this book.

♻ Enslow Publishers, Inc., is committed to printing our books on recycled paper. The paper in every book contains 10% to 30% post-consumer waste (PCW). The cover board on the outside of each book contains 100% PCW. Our goal is to do our part to help young people and the environment too!

Photo Credits: Alaskastock: Patrick Endres, p. 19, Ronald S. Phillips, p. 15, Steven Kazlowski, p. 8; Arcticphoto.com: © Wayne Lynch, pp. 2, 9; © 1999 Artville, LLC, p. 3; Corbis: © Darrell Gulen, p. 6, © Jenny E. Ross, pp. 1, 21; Getty Images: Michael S. Quinton, p. 16; Minden Pictures: Jim Brandenburg, pp. 12, 13, Michio Hoshino, p. 10, Patricio Robles Gil, p. 18, Winfried Wisniewski, p. 11, Yva Momatiuk & John Eastcott, pp. 7 (left), 23; naturepl.com: Eric Baccega, p. 20, Konstantin Mikhailov, pp. 2, 17, Philippe Clement, p. 5; NHPA: Mirko Stelzner, p. 14, Rich Kirchner, p. 7 (right).

Cover Photo: © Corbis/Jenny E. Ross

Enslow Elementary
an imprint of
E | **Enslow Publishers, Inc.**
40 Industrial Road
Box 398
Berkeley Heights, NJ 07922
USA
http://www.enslow.com